Wealth-Building with Renewable Energy
Future-Proof Strategies

Table of Contents

Chapter 1. Introduction

Special Report: "Wealth-Building with Renewable Energy: Future-Proof Strategies"

Get ready for a thrilling journey into a world bursting with opportunity – renewable energy! This Special Report is your gateway to understanding and capitalizing on a sector that's not only key to our planet's future but also brimming with financial potential. Imagine an adventure into a world where making money aligns seamlessly with making a difference. Our meticulously crafted guide, "Wealth-Building with Renewable Energy: Future-Proof Strategies," is designed to unlock the power of green energy for your wealth-building goals, connecting the dots between sustainability and profitability. By harnessing the power of the sun, wind, and water, you can foster a robust financial future for yourself while contributing to a sustainable and responsible world. This report comes loaded with insightful perspectives, practical tips, and captivating case studies that will stoke your enthusiasm and inspire you to take the plunge. Time to ride the green wave to a richer, more responsible future!

Chapter 2. Exploring the Scope of Renewable Energy

Renewable energy has engrossed worldwide attention over the past few decades due to its crucial role in offsetting the effects of global warming and climate change. This sector has undergone significant expansion and innovation, escalating its scope beyond expectation.

2.1. Rise of Renewable Energy

The modern age has seen a rampant increase in energy consumption. Traditional sources, such as oil, coal, and natural gas, contribute to a significant portion of this energy demand but at the cost of increased carbon emissions and environmental degradation. Renewable energy, in contrast, offers a resilient and environmentally conscious alternative.

Renewable sources like sunlight, wind, rain, tides, and geothermal heat are available in abundance, and leveraging them for energy production results in significantly fewer greenhouse gas emissions compared to burning fossil fuels. The rise in renewable energy is thus a testament to a global commitment towards a sustainable future.

2.2. Technological Spectrum of Renewable Energy

Technological advancements have amplified the realm of renewable energy. Key technologies that fall under this umbrella include solar power, wind energy, hydropower, bioenergy, and geothermal energy.

Solar power harnesses the energy of the sun. With solar photovoltaics and concentrated solar power systems, we can collect this energy and transform it into usable electricity. Despite the initial setup cost, the long-term benefits of solar systems in terms of both cost and environment are exceedingly promising.

Wind energy converts the kinetic energy in wind into electricity using wind turbines. It's a clean, low-cost, and readily available energy source with the potential for both onshore and offshore installations.

Hydropower, the earliest source of renewable energy, utilizes the flow of water to generate electricity. Hydropower systems range from small-scale installations for individual homes to massive dams powering entire communities.

Bioenergy encompasses utilizing organic materials (like agricultural and forest residues, algae, or waste) to produce energy-rich gas or liquid fuels. It even extends to producing electricity and heat.

Geothermal energy exploits heat trapped beneath the Earth's surface. While access and availability may be limiting factors, geothermal systems are long-lasting, reliable, and perfect for heating and cooling applications.

2.3. Market Growth and Investment Opportunities

There's no denying the market for renewable energy is burgeoning. With forecasts predicting that renewables will supply nearly 30% of global electricity demand by 2023, there has never been a more exciting time to invest in this sector. Solar and wind energy are becoming increasingly competitive with conventional sources, and the prospects for hydro, bioenergy, and geothermal power also appear rosy.

By investing in renewable energy projects, you're not just securing a sustainable future but also solidifying your financial prospects. Whether you opt for direct investments like buying stakes in renewable energy companies or indirect investments through mutual funds or ETFs, the opportunities are endless.

Furthermore, governments worldwide are offering incentives and subsidies to encourage clean energy use, thereby lowering the risk factor associated with such investments. Initiatives like carbon pricing, green bonds, and power purchase agreements further sweeten the deal for prospective investors.

2.4. Environmental and Socioeconomic Impact

The implications of renewable energy are not confined to the environment alone; they permeate social and economic realms too. Adopting renewable energy on a broader scale can cut down harmful emissions, improve public health, create jobs, and stimulate local economies.

With lower operational costs, renewables often translate into cheaper electricity, thereby benefiting consumers. Furthermore, renewable energy infrastructure requires human labor for installation, maintenance, and management, offering potential for job creation and local economic growth.

2.5. Geopolitical Aspects of Renewable Energy

Renewable energy also carries significant geopolitical weight. Countries with ample renewable resources can attain energy independence, reducing reliance on importing fossil fuels. This transition can strengthen national security, lower geopolitical risks, and provide these countries with a strategic advantage.

Countries with leading renewable energy industries can also export technology and expertise, fostering global partnerships for a sustainable future.

In summary, the scope of renewable energy is extensive and evolved, touching upon technological, economic, environmental, and geopolitical dimensions. This sector, with its immense potential and promising horizon, makes up an exciting avenue to explore, invest, and spur global change.

Chapter 3. The Economics of Green Power: A Deeper Dive

The renewable energy landscape is in a constant state of change, with the rapid development of technologies and policies shaping the economics of green power. This dynamic environment presents distinctive opportunities and challenges. Let this be your guiding star as we delve into the intricate factors driving renewable energy economics.

3.1. Understanding Renewable Energy Markets

The value of renewable energy largely derives from its relationship with energy markets. These markets function on three levels: the wholesale electricity market, the market for renewable energy certificates, and the market for carbon offsets. They intertwine and interact, creating complex dynamics that affect the profitability of renewable energy projects.

The wholesale electricity market refers to the platform where utilities and electricity retailers purchase electricity from power generators. Prices in this market fluctuate due to supply and demand conditions, typically increasing during periods of high electricity usage and decreasing as demand falls. Renewable energy producers can take part in this market and sell their electricity.

Renewable Energy Certificates (RECs) represent the environmental benefits of one megawatt-hour (MWh) of electricity generated from renewable energy sources. These certificates can trade independently of the actual electricity, allowing corporations to buy RECs to meet sustainability goals, even if they don't directly consume the renewable energy. RECs provide an extra income stream for renewable energy producers besides selling electricity.

Carbon offsets are another integrated part of the renewable energy economic puzzle. Organizations can reduce their carbon footprint by purchasing carbon offsets, which are certificates that represent a reduction of one metric ton of greenhouse gas emissions. These certificates fund projects that reduce emissions, including renewables.

Understanding these markets and their dynamics is critical when venturing into renewable energy. The revenues from selling electricity, RECs, and carbon offsets form the backbone of a renewable energy project's business model.

3.2. Cost of Generation

The cost of generating power is a pivotal factor affecting the economics of renewable energy. It is crucial to delineate between capital costs and operating costs when considering a renewable energy project.

Capital costs or upfront costs of renewable energy technologies have witnessed significant reductions over the past decade, driving the surge in renewable energy installations. Costs related to site preparation, permits, and interconnection also form part of capital costs.

Operating costs include maintenance, insurance, and any costs associated with the administration of the renewable energy installation. In many instances, renewable energy technologies have lower operational expenditures than fossil fuel-based ones, mainly because they don't have fuel costs.

The levelized cost of electricity (LCOE) is a frequently used metric to compare different energy technologies. It represents the average total cost to build and operate a power-generating asset (like a solar panel or wind turbine) per unit of total electricity generated over the asset's life.

3.3. Policy Implications

Government policy plays a crucial role in shaping the economics of renewable energy. Policies aimed at reducing greenhouse gas emissions, encouraging clean energy development, or de-incentivizing fossil fuels have direct economic implications.

For instance, feed-in tariffs (FITs) and power purchase agreements (PPAs) guarantee a fixed payment to generators of renewable energy for their electricity output, ensuring revenue stability. Tax incentives such as the Investment Tax Credit (ITC) in the U.S. can reduce the capital cost of renewable energy projects, making them more competitive.

However, policy volatility can present risks to projects with long timescales, like renewable energy installations. Observing policy trends and advocating for supportive regulations where possible can effectively manage these risks.

3.4. Investment Opportunities

Renewable energy is a burgeoning investment sector attracting a diversity of stakeholders from individual investors to global corporations. Investment opportunities range from directly owning renewable energy projects to purchasing stocks or funds in renewable energy companies.

For direct project ownership, understanding the previously discussed factors such as energy markets, cost generation, and policy implications will be critical.

Investing in renewable energy stocks or funds provides investors the option to support renewable energy without taking on the responsibilities and risks of owning a project. Performance of these stocks and funds is influenced by broader market dynamics, policies, and the success of individual companies or projects.

3.5. Grid Integration

Successfully integrating renewable energy into the power grid is an economic challenge and opportunity. Balancing the intermittent supply of solar and wind energy with demand can be expensive. However, solutions such as energy storage and demand response programs present opportunities for business and innovation, alongside the growth of renewable energy.

In conclusion, while the future of renewable energy is bright, navigating its economics requires an understanding of the energy markets, costs, policy implications, investment opportunities, and challenges of grid integration. With this knowledge in hand, your path toward a profitable and sustainable future with renewable energy becomes clearer.

Chapter 4. Unlocking Solar Potential: Wealth in Sunlight

The sun beams an astonishing amount of energy to Earth every moment. According to the National Renewable Energy Laboratory (NREL), the potential solar energy that could be harnessed amounts to more than 1000 times our current global energy consumption. As an investor or entrepreneur, understanding how to tap into this energy source is paramount. With careful navigation, the renewable energy landscape can turn into a field of opportunity, enabling you to not only generate wealth but also make a difference in the fight against climate change.

4.1. Understanding Solar Energy: A Brief Overview

Solar power utilizes advanced technology known as photovoltaics (PV) to transform sunlight directly into electricity. In a nutshell, a solar PV system operates by allowing particles of light, or photons, to knock electrons free from atoms, creating a stream of electricity.

Recent innovations in design and materials have led to increasingly efficient solar collection and conversion, resulting in falling costs and rising accessibility. To put it simply, it's never been easier or more affordable to tap into the wealth of solar energy.

However, there's more to solar energy than merely installing panels. By recognizing and understanding the breadth and depth of the solar power industry, you can identify diverse investment opportunities to expand your wealth-building avenues. From small-scale residential installations, commercial applications to vast utility-scale developments, solar power offers a swath of possibilities.

4.2. Green Fields: Identifying Solar Market Opportunities

Incorporating solar into grid electricity is the most obvious way to harness this renewable energy source. Nevertheless, there is a variety of other ways entrepreneurs and investors can participate in this growing market:

+ **Residential:** The installation of solar panel systems on residential properties is a common way for households to access solar power. Moreover, it is one area that continues to grow in most developed countries, representing opportunity for investment and commercial engagement.

+ **Commercial & Industrial:** Businesses and industries are increasingly turning to solar energy to power their operations. From on-site solar arrays to buying solar power through a Power Purchase Agreement (PPA), these sectors present lucrative opportunities for wealth creation.

+ **Utility-Scale:** Utility-scale solar refers to large-scale solar power plants that deliver electricity to the grid. These projects typically range from 1 megawatt (MW) to several hundred MW and can generate substantial returns over long periods.

+ **Storage and batteries:** The solar industry doesn't stop at power generation. As the production of solar energy increases, so does the need for energy storage. Solar energy storage using batteries is a rapidly expanding sector that is driving significant investor interest.

Looking at our world through a solar lens provides a fresh perspective on wealth-building, opening opportunities that extend beyond traditional investment avenues.

4.3. Investing in Solar Stocks: High-Potential Picks

Investing in solar energy stocks could prove beneficial for those looking for a more hands-off approach to wealth-building in the renewables sector. However, like any investment, it's crucial to do your due diligence before taking the plunge. Here are some areas to consider:

+ **Manufacturers:** These companies produce the actual solar panels that outfit homes, businesses, and large-scale solar farms. Given the increasing demand, investing in manufacturers can provide excellent returns.

+ **Installers:** These firms install solar systems on residential, commercial, and utility-scale facilities. As more people adopt solar, the market for professional installation services is expanding.

+ **Providers of ancillary services:** This broad category includes companies involved in various stages of the solar supply chain – from makers of inverters and other critical solar components to those involved in finance, insurance, and consulting services for solar projects.

+ **Utility companies:** Numerous utility companies have deployed solar power. Investing in these utility companies might be an indirect but effective way to grow your wealth in the solar sector.

Knowing where and how to invest isn't always a straightforward task. Thorough research, professional advice, and, above all, patience, can lead to fruitful results.

4.4. Solar Energy Around the Globe: A Comparative Analysis

Combining investment opportunities with a broader awareness of the global solar landscape can foster a more strategic approach to wealth-building. Analyzing solar energy adoption, policy landscape, and market trends around the world can help identify hotspots for potential investment.

For instance, China is currently leading the world in terms of installed solar power capacity, followed by the United States, Japan, and Germany. Emerging markets like India and various countries in Africa and South America are spearheading the development of solar energy.

4.5. Solar Regulatory Landscape: Understanding the Implications

A comprehensive grasp of the regulatory landscape overseeing the renewable industry is crucial for successful participation in the solar sector. This knowledge can give an investor or entrepreneur an upper hand in anticipating challenges and capitalizing on incentives.

Governmental policies on renewables, subsidies, tax incentives, feed-in tariffs, and renewable portfolio standards differ by country and can significantly impact the viability and profitability of solar projects.

Chapter 5. Final Thoughts: Lighting the Way to Wealth

Solar energy stands to play a significant role in our global energy future. For the savvy investor or entrepreneur, the dawn of this new era holds immense promise. The journey to wealth-building with solar energy isn't always easy, but with the right knowledge, strategy, and commitment, it offers an avenue to create substantial wealth while contributing to a sustainable future.

Investing in solar power not only potentially generates financial returns, but it also contributes to a cleaner planet. As the world continues to pivot towards renewable energy, investors who understand and capitalize on the solar sector's promise will find themselves at the forefront of building wealth sustainably – truly, a golden opportunity bathed in sunlight.

Chapter 6. Wind Energy: Profiting from the Invisible Power

Our in-depth exploration into harnessing the power of the incorporeal yet potent force that is wind energy begins with a touch of history. Wind has been serving humankind since early civilization; from propelling ships across oceans to powering windmills for milling grain. But the true power of wind lies in its ability to generate power, electrical power, that can light up cities, fuel economies, and redefine power generation processes.

6.1. Harvesting The Invisible: Understanding Wind Power

To take full advantage of wind energy, it's essential to understand what it is and how it's harnessed. Wind energy is a form of solar energy. Wind formations are influenced by the uneven heating of the atmosphere by the sun, irregularities of the earth's surface, and the rotation of the earth. Wind flow, or kinetic energy, when "harvested" by wind turbines, can provide power to generate electricity.

Simply put, a wind turbine functions the antithesis of a fan. Instead of electricity powering a fan to make wind, the wind powers the turbine to create electricity. The energy in the wind transforms into mechanical power, powering a generator that converts it to electrical energy.

6.2. The Wind Market: Investment Landscape

As an investor keeping an eye on the market, you will recognize that the wind energy sector is vast and rich in opportunity – and it's expanding rapidly. In the past decade, wind energy has become one of the cheapest sources of electricity, surpassing even the traditional fossil fuel sources in many markets. Furthermore, technological advancements and efficiency improvements have led to higher capacity and thus, a higher return on investments.

According to the Global Wind Energy Council (GWEC), 93 GW of new capacity was installed in 2020 alone. This is a 53% year-on-year increase, illustrating the aggressive growth and lucrative prospect of the wind power market.

Bloomberg New Energy Finance also projects that the total investment in wind power would reach $5.3 trillion by 2040. This projection tells us that the wind energy market is ripe for investors looking to build wealth while encouraging a renewable and sustainable future.

6.3. Choosing The Right Winds: Key Factors

Investing in wind energy is not as simple as pouring money into the first wind-related opportunity you see. Key factors come into play in determining the potential and viability of a wind energy project. Knowledge of these variables can help determine the profitability of an investment.

1. **Wind Speed and Consistency**: The amount of energy a wind turbine can harness is directly proportional to the cube of its wind speed. Hence, even a slight increase in wind speed can lead

to significantly higher energy production.

2. **Site selection**: Site selection comprises factors like accessibility, proximity to electrical grids, local demand for electricity, and most importantly, wind resource assessment.

3. **Turbine technology**: Technological advancements and the efficiency of the turbine used also determine the profitability of a wind energy project.

4. **Policy and regulatory environment**: Policies and incentives for renewable energy by local or national government, as well as legal and environmental constraints, significantly impact the feasibility and profitability of a wind energy project.

5. **Economic factors**: Economic aspects such as initial capital costs, ongoing operational costs, energy price, and potential incentives/taxes also determine a project's financial viability.

6.4. Investment Avenues: Portfolio Diversification

There are multiple avenues through which one can invest in wind energy:

1. **Stocks**: One can invest in stocks of wind energy companies, wind turbine manufacturers, or even companies that supply critical components to these manufacturers.

2. **ETFs (Exchange Traded Funds)**: These financial instruments track the performance of a specific index or sector, such as renewable energy. ETFs offer diversification and lessen the risk associated with investing in individual stocks.

3. **Mutual Funds**: There are many mutual funds that focus specifically on renewable energy, offering another excellent diversification strategy.

4. **Direct investment**: For those who have the means and the

inclination, directly investing in a wind farm can be an attractive opportunity.

5. **Green Bonds**: Bonds issued by government or corporations to raise capital for renewable energy projects. They offer a fixed return over time.

6.5. Conclusion: Believing in the Invisible Power

When it comes to investing in wind energy, the aim should not be 'quick profits'. Instead, it is about recognizing the shifting global dynamic towards renewable energy. Investing in wind energy lets you participate in that shift towards a greener, more sustainable future—and profit from it. As they say in the green industry, "It's not just the climate that's changing."

So, treat this guide as your wind vane, directing you where the "investment winds" are blowing. Tune in to the shifts in the market and let the invisible force guide your sails towards a prosperous and sustainable financial future. Remember, it is said that the best time to plant a tree was 20 years ago, the second-best time is now. The same logic applies to investing in our green future. The future is windy, and it bodes well.

Chapter 7. The Rise of Hydro: Opportunities in Water

Water has been a source of power since time immemorial. Our ancestors relied on it for their day-to-day lives, using its sheer kinetic force to grind grains or move heavy loads. Today, we have channeled this element's power into a more sophisticated form – hydroelectric power. Wielded properly, this renewable resource presents vast opportunities for investors seeking both fiscal growth and positive environmental influence.

7.1. The Basics of Hydroelectric Power

Hydroelectric power, or 'hydro,' harnesses water's kinetic energy. Broadly, this process includes the construction of massive dams that hold back and control large bodies of water. When released, the water flows forcefully through turbines, spinning blades that drive a generator to produce electricity.

While hydroelectric power may seem relatively modern, it's an ancient practice updated with new technology. Water wheels, used for millennia to grind grain into flour, represent a type of manual hydroelectric power. Today's hydroelectric dams are just a bigger, more sophisticated evolution of this ancient technology.

7.2. Why Invest in Hydroelectric Power?

Hydroelectric power's primary appeal lies in its capacity for producing substantial amounts of clean, renewable energy. The setup is exhaustless – as long as there's flowing water, the potential for electricity generation exists. For investors, this offers the enticing prospect of continuous output and potentially consistent returns.

Moreover, hydroelectric power is scalable. From small turbines providing energy for a handful of homes to towering dams powering whole cities, there's a place for hydroelectric investments of all sizes.

Further bolstering hydro's investment potential is that, unlike some renewable technologies, it comes with a proven track record. Countries such as Norway and Canada extensively rely upon hydroelectric energy, contributing to their energy matrix and showcasing hydro's viability at scale.

7.3. The Versatility of Small Hydropower

Big isn't always best. In the world of hydroelectric power, smaller projects known as 'small hydropower' play a crucial role and generate ample opportunity for potential investors.

Unlike large dams, small hydropower projects are built on a modest scale. They often require fewer resources, create less environmental disruption, and yield an immediate return on investment. As developing nations embrace renewables, the demand for small hydropower solutions is set to rise, further highlighting the potential benefits for investors.

Also, small hydropower projects are frequently constructed in isolated or off-grid locations. In these areas, small hydropower can yield considerable profits, making them increasingly appealing to investors who sense the change in tides for the power sector.

7.4. Risks and Considerations

Like all investments, hydroelectric power investment comes with risks. Environmental, regulatory, and socio-economic variables all play a part in a project's viability and profit-generating potential.

Large dam projects, while capable of producing considerable electricity, can have significant environmental impacts and face increasingly stringent regulations. Additionally, such projects often involve substantial amounts of capital and lengthy construction timescales, which could prolong initial payback periods for investors.

Moreover, both large-scale and small-scale hydro projects can be affected by climate change, with shifts in precipitation patterns potentially impacting power generation. Thus, investors must thoroughly consider these risks before diving into the hydroelectric sector.

7.5. Current Trends and Future Possibilities

Despite the challenges, the future of hydroelectric power investment seems bright. Global initiatives to reduce carbon emissions motivate countries, especially developing nations, towards renewable energy sources like hydro. The increased demand for clean, reliable energy, combined with hydro's proven capacity, signifies a probable growth trend for this sector.

Moreover, technological innovations continue to drive the hydroelectric power industry's efficiency and productivity. The advent of 'pumped storage' - a method of storing energy by using two water reservoirs at different heights - offers intriguing prospects for future power storage, enhancing hydro's attractiveness as an investment opportunity.

In conclusion, the journey of hydroelectric power is far from over. From ancient waterwheels to modern dams, the transformative power of water continues to shape our world, presenting plenty of opportunities for an enterprising investor. The rewards? A potential steady stream of returns and the satisfaction of contributing to the world's sustainability efforts.

Chapter 8. Bioenergy and Wealth Creation: Growing Assets

Bioenergy, a renewable energy source derived from living or recently living materials, provides an unparalleled opportunity to build your financial future. With its myriad applications from transportation to electricity generation, bioenergy offers an attractive pathway to both environmental stewardship and wealth creation. A look into bioenergy's potential will reveal its value as a versatile and efficient source of energy, making it an enticing asset in your wealth-building portfolio.

8.1. Bioenergy Basics

To appreciate the investment potential that bioenergy offers, it's important to first understand what it is. Bioenergy is energy derived from biomass, i.e., organic materials. These feedstocks for bioenergy production come in a plethora of forms, such as agricultural residues, forestry products, and various waste products from industrial processes. Even algae, a simple water-dwelling organism, can be a source of bioenergy.

In transforming these resources into power, bioenergy technologies come into play. For instance, bioheat systems burn biomass directly to generate heat. There are also biopower technologies that convert biomass into electricity, such as combustion, gasification, and anaerobic digestion. On another front, biofuels like biodiesel and bioethanol are generated through conversion processes such as fermentation and esterification.

For perspective: in 2020, bioenergy accounted for about 5% of the total global primary energy production—more than wind, solar, and hydroelectric power combined.

8.2. Why Invest in Bioenergy?

Bioenergy presents an intriguing opportunity for investors due to its versatility, scalability, and potential for significant returns. This renewable energy source stands as one of the few renewables that offer a solution for multiple energy sectors: heat, electricity, and transport fuels. Unlike other renewables, bioenergy has the advantage of being storable and transportable, making it a tantalizing solution for providing reliable renewable energy.

There's also tremendous growth potential. As global energy consumption rises, the International Energy Agency projects that bioenergy will account for 30% of growth in renewable energy consumption through to 2023. That statistic alone tells a story of a growing sector ripe for investment.

8.3. The Economics of Bioenergy

Bioenergy economically contributes to communities by generating jobs, fostering new business development, and reducing waste treatment costs. Furthermore, as bioenergy is derived from a diverse set of feedstocks which are locally available, it promotes energy security and reduces the reliance on fossil fuels.

Various economic models have revealed the financial viability and profitability of the bioenergy sector. For instance, the U.S. Department of Energy estimates that for every quadrillion British thermal units (BTUs) of bioenergy produced, $130-460 million can be generated in economic activities, supporting 8000-25000 jobs.

The bioenergy market is further buoyed by favorable policies and incentives introduced by governments worldwide. These include tax credits, subsidies, and renewable portfolio standards, all of which encourage investment and add to the economic attractiveness of bioenergy projects.

8.4. Case Study: Danske Commodities Powering Wealth With Bioenergy

As an investor, seeing real-world examples of wealth creation via bioenergy can provide insight into the potential return of bioenergy ventures. Danske Commodities, a Denmark-based energy trading company, is a case in point.

In 2017, Danske Commodities invested heavily in bioenergy, purchasing three combined heat and power plants in the U.K. that generate electricity from biomass. This move paid off handsomely—in 2018, the company's operating profit increased by 43% to €60 million, largely due to its bioenergy operations.

More importantly, this once small trading company has evolved into a leading player in Europe's energy markets. Danske Commodities shows that investing in renewable energy can lay the groundwork for monumental financial growth.

8.5. Investing in Bioenergy: A Step-by-Step Guide

Investing in bioenergy might seem intimidating, especially if you're new to renewable energy. However, when broken down into steps, it's a journey you can undertake with confidence.

1. Identify Your Investment Objectives: Are you looking for long-term growth or short-term gains? Your goals will shape the type of bioenergy investments you should pursue.

2. Research the Market: Understanding the market is critical to successful investing. Look at bioenergy trends, the political climate, and economic indicators.

3. Assess The Risks: All investments carry risks. Evaluate potential risks, and consider insurance and risk mitigation strategies.

4. Diversify: Don't put all your eggs in one basket. Consider investing in different areas of the bioenergy sector.

5. Seek Professional Advice: Lastly, don't go it alone. Engage with financial advisors and energy experts to help navigate your investment journey.

Wealth-building through bioenergy can be an exciting and rewarding endeavor. It holds the promise of not only generating impressive returns, but also empowering economic development, fostering jobs, and contributing to a greener, more sustainable world. And that's a future worth investing in.

Chapter 9. Geothermal Energy: Capitalizing on the Earth's Heat

The heat from the earth provides an energy source that is not only endless but also often underestimated. Known as geothermal energy, this source continues to serve as a foundation for renewable energy development. With recent technological advancements, there has never been a more opportune time to utilize this wealth-building resource.

9.1. Understanding Geothermal Energy

Geothermal energy comes directly from the earth's internal heat. This organic thermal energy is naturally produced by radioactive decay and continuous heat loss from the earth's formation. Around 20% of this energy is from residual heat, while the rest comes from the decay of naturally radioactive isotopes. This internal heat is constant and practically limitless, making it an inviting potential for wealth-building.

Deep underground, earth's temperature can reach over 5,000 degrees Celsius – as hot as the sun's surface. To put this overwhelming nature of underground heat into perspective, if only 0.1% of the thermal energy found beneath the earth's crust, just to the depth of 10 km, could be harnessed, it would cater to over 20,000 times the yearly total consumption of energy worldwide!

9.2. Extracting Geothermal Energy

There are various methods to harness geothermal energy, based on the depth one digs into the earth:

- Surface geothermal energy: The shallow ground, upto 400 meters deep, maintains a nearly constant temperature – above freezing during the winter and below our body temperature in the summer.

- Deep and ultra-deep geothermal energy: This involves depths beyond 400 meters, all the way to 10 kilometers. The energy harvesting increases the deeper one gets, with temperatures skyrocketing to several hundred degrees Celsius.

Several technologies used to extract geothermal energy, regardless of the depth, include:

1. Geothermal power plants: These plants use steam produced from reservoirs of hot water found a few kilometers or more below the earth's surface. There are three types: dry steam, flash steam and binary cycle power plants.

2. Ground-source heat pumps: Homes and businesses use these pumps, which take advantage of the constant temperatures near the surface to heat buildings in the winter and cool them in the summer.

3. Direct use and district heating systems: These systems take advantage of shallow reservoirs to provide heat for residences and commercial establishments.

9.3. The Financial Aspects

Harnessing the earth's heat as a source of power is an exciting prospect for wealth-building. The geothermal energy market is projected to grow at a compound annual growth rate (CAGR) of 5.9%

from 2020 to 2040, estimated to reach $23.5 billion value by 2040.

Moreover, the cost of geothermal energy production has been steadily declining. The levelized cost of electricity (LCOE) generated from a typical geothermal power plant is less than that of a coal-fired power plant, a natural gas power plant, and even falls within the price range of large photovoltaic solar power panels, depending on the project's location and scale.

This decline in cost potentially translates to higher profit margins for investors, promising a compelling return on investment. As countries strive to achieve energy independence and lower carbon footprints, governments are offering incentives and subsidies for renewable energy projects, including those exploring geothermal energy, making it even more financially attractive.

9.4. Risks and Challenges

Like any investment opportunity, geothermal energy also presents risks and challenges. These include high upfront costs for plant construction, potential for reservoir depletion over time, location dependence, and concerns about greenhouse gas emissions. However, technological advancements, improved laws and regulations, and progressive climate policies are gradually mitigating these risks.

9.5. Investing in Geothermal Energy

Investing in geothermal energy is unique because it involves backing a sustainable power source that's capable of providing energy around the clock, irrespective of weather conditions. This reliability often translates to consistent revenue streams, making it a viable option for becoming part of your diversified clean energy portfolio.

Other than investing in geothermal power plant projects, one can consider buying stocks of companies involved in geothermal energy production. One can also diversify risk by investing in mutual funds or exchange-traded funds (ETFs) concentrating on renewable energy.

Bear in mind, before investing, thorough research into potential projects is crucial. Look at not only the potential returns, but also the company's management, strategies, and track record in the geothermal energy sector.

9.6. Conclusion

While it's an underutilized source now, the role of geothermal energy in our energy mix is set to increase significantly in the years to come. With a careful investment approach, you can capitalize on this wealth-building opportunity and contribute to creating a sustainable future. Geothermal energy offers the potential for truly sustainable wealth – wealth that's not merely about financial gain but also about contributing positively to the world. Prospective investors now stand at the threshold of this exciting, profitable realm, and with the right tools and knowledge, can seize the opportunities it brings.

Chapter 10. Driving Financial Success with Electric Vehicles

The future of private transport appears destined to be electric. Given this, we can confidently anticipate that electric vehicles (EVs) represent a significant investment opportunity. EVs are reshaping automotive industry and urban transportation paradigms globally, propelled by technological breakthroughs like improved battery technology and attractive government incentives.

10.1. Market Overview and Investment Rationale

The economics of electric vehicles are exciting. Their market share is growing steadily, a trend projected to accelerate due to advancements in electrical infrastructure, battery technology, manufacturing efficiencies, policy support, social conscience, and totality of ownership costs.

From an investment perspective, this burgeoning sector presents opportunities across the supply chain, from natural resource extraction to vehicle manufacturing and public charging stations. Namely, a shift toward developing and adopting renewable energy sources, enhancing storage capabilities, and building necessary infrastructures can open doors to investors looking for environmentally sustainable and financially rewarding opportunities.

A study by Bloomberg NEF forecasts that by 2040, 57% of all passenger vehicle sales, and over 30% of the global passenger vehicle fleet, will be electric. This market growth is likely to profoundly impact associated industries, offering a decade-long expansion landscape for shrewd investors.

10.2. EVs and The Battery Revolution

The greatest challenge and opportunity in the electric vehicle revolution lies in the battery. A vehicle's range and price depend significantly on its battery. Lithium-ion batteries, currently the industry standard, have seen dramatic cost reductions, from $1,100 per kWh in 2010 to around $137 in 2020, making EVs increasingly affordable.

Key components in these batteries include lithium, cobalt, nickel, and graphite — investments in the extraction and refining of these raw materials could pay dividends. For instance, lithium, a soft, white metal used in various battery chemistries, is experiencing steadily growing demand. If you're looking to invest in a 'picks and shovels' manner, exploration and mining companies servicing this demand could deserve a place in your portfolio.

10.3. Charging Infrastructure: Powering the Future

A vital aspect of EV adoption is the availability of reliable charging infrastructure. As EVs continue to proliferate, the demand for equipment manufacturers, installation services, and utility providers is set to increase.

Many governments are actively supporting EV charging infrastructure, with initiatives such as grants, tax credits, and regulations that mandate installation in buildings. Infrastructure-focused ESG (Environmental, Social, Governance) funds or stocks like ChargePoint (CHPT), Blink Charging (BLNK), or EVBox could offer viable investment routes.

Furthermore, utilities stand to gain from the growing need for electricity. Their involvement ranges from generating and selling more electricity to owning and operating charging stations. Utilities that can demonstrate a commitment to incorporating and facilitating renewable energy sources are particularly attractive.

10.4. Vehicle Manufacturing: More Than Just Tesla

While Tesla's high-profile successes have put it in the spotlight, it's far from the only game in town. Traditional automakers, like General Motors and Volkswagen, are transitioning towards EVs, announcing multi-billion dollar investment plans.

Investing in such players, or those who supply parts to them, is another method to profit from the EV surge. Several EV-specific exchange-traded funds (ETFs) such as Global X Autonomous & Electric Vehicles ETF (DRIV) or iShares Self-Driving EV and Tech ETF (IDRV) provide broad exposure to this sector.

10.5. The Future Looks Bright

The global transition to electric vehicles presents an electric future. It offers multiple avenues for investors wishing to participate in this revolution while contributing towards mitigating climate change. As we have seen, the opportunities are plentiful, diverse, and accessible. Investment in electric vehicles allows for not just financial gain, but a chance to directly influence and contribute to a transformative global shift towards sustainability and clean transportation.

EVs represent a balancing act between profit and responsibility. As investors, we have the chance to capitalize on a sector that represents a profound shift in our approach to personal and public transportation, moving towards a future where driving is clean, sustainable, and ultimately, electric. This shift represents an opportunity to build wealth while contributing to protecting our planet—a win-win proposition, and a fitting contribution to this adventure.

With the information and future-proof strategies outlined in this chapter, you now have a comprehensive understanding of the transformative potential of electric vehicles and how they can drive financial success. You are poised to build your wealth by investing wisely and thoughtfully in this unprecedented transition towards a more sustainable future.

Chapter 11. Creating Your Investment Strategy: Real-world Case Studies

When it comes to creating your investment strategy in the realm of renewable energy, let's dive into some real-world case studies. They hold a wealth of practical insights, serving as a guide along the treacherous path between enthusiasm and actual investment success.

11.1. The Turnkey Solar Solution

Let's begin with John, a smart investor from California who recognized early on the potential of solar power. John chose what's called a turnkey solar investment. A turnkey operation is one that's ready to use, it requires no additional work beyond its initial setup. In the realm of solar power, it refers to a fully functional, ready-to-use solar farm from day one.

John purchased a ready-made solar farm in Southern California through a company specializing in developing such projects. He was part of the growth of larger-scale solar farms, rapidly increasing renewable energy capacity. His initial investment – a hefty sum of $1M – was steep, but due to his strategic positioning and foresight, John was able to reap the benefits sooner than later.

His key return metrics: . Net Energy Metering (NEM), which allows him to earn credits for excess energy fed back into the grid. . A 30% federal Investment Tax Credit (ITC), further sweetening the deal. . An ongoing revenue stream via Power Purchase Agreements (PPAs) with local utilities.

This case demonstrates the substantial returns that investment in solar energy can yield. It does require a significant upfront financial injection, but that is usually offset by the robust earning potential over time if the right due diligence, tax planning, and contracts come into play.

11.2. Breaking Wind – Turbines that is!

Our next story brings us to Mary, an investor based in Texas. Mary saw Texas's wind energy potential and decided to take a more hands-on, long-term approach. She purchased land with high wind potential and invested in several high-capacity wind turbines. Also, she chartered an energy company to manage and distribute the power generated.

Her initial investment was around $2M. This sum included the cost of the land, wind turbines, setup, and company charter. However, the circumstances favored Mary's move. Texas stands in a strategic position regarding wind energy owing to its vast, windy plains and supportive local regulations.

Mary's key return metrics included: . Energy production sold to utility companies under a long-term PPA. . Federal tax credits available for wind energy production. . Increased land value due to the wind farm.

Despite the higher initial investment and slow start, Mary's wind energy venture is generating a steady profit. This case clearly illustrates that geographical considerations, proper planning, and patience can lead to a successful investment in the renewable energy sector.

11.3. Small Scale Hydropower Excitement

Finally, let's consider George, an entrepreneur from Colorado, serious about sustainability. George opted for a small-scale hydroelectric power plant using a stream running through his property. He invested approximately $300,000 in setting up the plant, including getting the appropriate permits.

George's key return metrics: . Selling power back to the local grid (Net Energy Metering). . The increasing value of his property due to the plant. . Federal and state-level tax benefits for green energy production.

George's case reveals an interesting facet of renewable energy investment: the potential to reap profit from under-utilized assets, such as a small stream.

In conclusion, our real-world case studies offer priceless lessons. They showcase sustainable wealth-building via investment in the renewable energy sector isn't a far-off dream but an achievable reality. Core lessons include understanding returns from various sources (energy sales, tax benefits, property value), thorough due diligence, and not hesitating to seek professional help. Remember, though, your individual circumstances, appetite for risk, and access to resources will determine the appropriate investment strategy. Seize the day, and harness the power of renewable energy for profitable, future-proof investments.

Chapter 12. Future Trends: Mapping Your Sustainable Financial Journey

Understanding the current trends and envisaging the future requires gaining an intimate knowledge of the renewable energy landscape. It involves delving deep into the world of renewables, the technologies that are shaping it, and the policies that fuel it.

12.1. Unfolding Renewable Landscape

With the growing awareness of climate change and its drastic implications, planet Earth is witnessing an unprecedented paradigm shift - a transition from nonrenewable to renewable energy sources. The renewable energy industry, comprising mainly solar, wind, hydropower, and bioenergy, is playing a vital role in delivering electricity across the world, reducing greenhouse gas emissions and making energy consumption and production sustainable and humane.

Solar energy, the planet's most abundant energy source, is taking giant strides forward. The cost of solar photovoltaic (PV) power has plunged dramatically, making it an exciting sector for wealth creation. The annual PV installations are set to double by 2030, indicating a bright future.

From powering homes to fuelling industries, wind energy is proving to be a reliable solution to meet energy needs while maintaining a low carbon footprint. Wind turbine technology has evolved, making wind farms more productive and cost-effective. Additionally, the emerging offshore wind sector has been showing a skyrocketing trajectory, attracting hefty investments.

Hydro and bioenergy have been traditional players in the renewable sector. However, they have evolved far beyond powering watermills and wood-fired stoves. Today, they offer manifold investment opportunities, from modern bioenergy projects to sophisticated hydroelectric power plants.

12.2. Progressive Policies Fuelling The Sector

The global political environment supporting renewable energy has ushered numerous legislative changes and incentives encouraging individuals and companies to invest in the sector.

An array of green initiatives and policies have been introduced throughout the world, aimed at fostering the renewable sector. Incentives such as Feed-in Tariffs (FiTs), Power Purchase Agreements (PPAs), tax benefits, and grants can result in substantial returns on your green investments.

This positive political environment has spurred the exponential growth of the renewable sector, making it a hotspot for both novice and seasoned investors.

12.3. Harnessing Technology and Innovation

Artificial Intelligence, Machine Learning, and Internet of Things have found their place in the renewable energy sector. Emerging technologies are optimizing energy generation, increasing efficiency, and reducing costs of operation. Predictive maintenance, smart grids, and energy storage technologies, to name a few, are revolutionizing the way we produce and consume energy.

These technological advancements not only make renewable energy sources more appealing but also increase the potential for higher returns on your investments.

12.4. Investment Opportunities

Renewable energy presents a myriad of investment opportunities, making it possible for anyone, anywhere, at any time, to start a journey towards sustainable wealth creation.

You could invest directly in renewable energy projects or companies specializing in renewable energy production. For those interested in less direct involvement, green bonds and green funds offer an excellent way to invest in a diverse portfolio of green projects without the hassle of direct management. Further, public equities investing in renewable energy-focused companies present a good opportunity for growing wealth.

For the entrepreneurial minded, starting a renewable energy venture could turn out to be a gold mine. With the right business model and strategic planning, such a venture can thrive in the booming renewable energy market.

12.5. Planning For Future

As you embark on your journey towards building wealth with renewable energy, it's essential to be patient and persistent. Long term investments in this sector are often the most profitable. The returns on investment in the renewable energy sector often see a significant spike after an initial period of progress and development.

Educate yourself on current trends, stay updated about the latest technological advancements, and understand the different aspects of renewable energy policies, speaking with an experienced advisor if necessary. These steps can together help you build a sustainable and robust investment portfolio in the renewable energy sector.

So whether you are a seasoned investor or a novice, the renewable energy sector is replete with opportunities to build wealth while contributing to a greener, cleaner planet. As the saying goes, "The best time to plant a tree was twenty years ago. The second best time is now." It's time to sow the seeds of your greener investments!